This is our...

Happy
Anniversary

...Perennial Cardbook

anthony j. gribin

ISBN No. 97809827376-3-7
first edition

TTGpress

Our names are:

The date we were married is:

Introduction

Your anniversary CardBook is an instant time capsule! The idea behind it is to gather well-wishes from people that care about you, over a long period of time. One of the two of you (spouse, partner or signifigant other) gave this to the other, but it belongs to you both. It is similar to an autograph book at graduation; except the event of note is your anniversary.

The more people that enter notes the better, and the more years the book is used, the better. Over time, you will be able to gauge how your children have matured as their entries change from bare legibility to adult sophistication; from stick figures to Rembrandt. Your CardBook should be brought out when you celebrate your anniversary, and all attending encouraged to sign.

The Cardbook will be "retired" after the celebration, put on a shelf, and "unretired" when the next anniversary rolls around.

There are 101 blank pages in each CardBook. 100 plus one for good luck. On the top of each page, you will see, "This is our____ Anniversary, celebrated in ____." Enter the appropriate numbers, such as "12th" and "2014," to indicate that you celebrated your 12th anniversary in 2014. It is unlikely that you will run out of room, yet it is possible if one or more celebrations are attended by, and the book is written in by, many people. Use as many pages as necessary for each anniversary.

The CardBook can serve other purposes as well. Pictures of you as a couple can be pasted into the book each year. Annotations, either humorous or serious can be added. For example, "Aunt Sally was bombed when she wrote this," or "This was the last anniversary that Dad was able to attend." You can make notes about who attended and where the celebration occurred. You can also mark down other happy occasions through the year, such as graduations, family births or promotions.

This CardBook may replace individual yearly cards that, though they are nice to read in the moment, generally just collect dust afterwards until they are tossed to save space. Further, the often trite messages contained in store-bought cards cannot compare with a thoughtful and personal note written to you by the person who is closest to you. Reading "You mean more to me than ever..." written by your husband or wife is a lot more meaningful than reading it in a printed card. And by limiting the number of cards bought over the years, you will save money (on the cards themselves and the gas used to go to purchase them) and spare a few trees in the process.

After even one year of entries by multiple well-wishers, your CardBook will become an instant keepsake. It will aid remembrance of how you celebrated your anniversaries, who was there to share it with the two of you and how the years have changed everyone. It is also a legacy for the next generation, to be put in the same category as old picture albums, videos and family trees. And, by the way, HAPPY ANNIVERSARY!

This is our ____ Anniversary, celebrated in ____

This is our ____ Anniversary, celebrated in ____

This is our ____ Anniversary, celebrated in ____

This is our ____ Anniversary, celebrated in ____

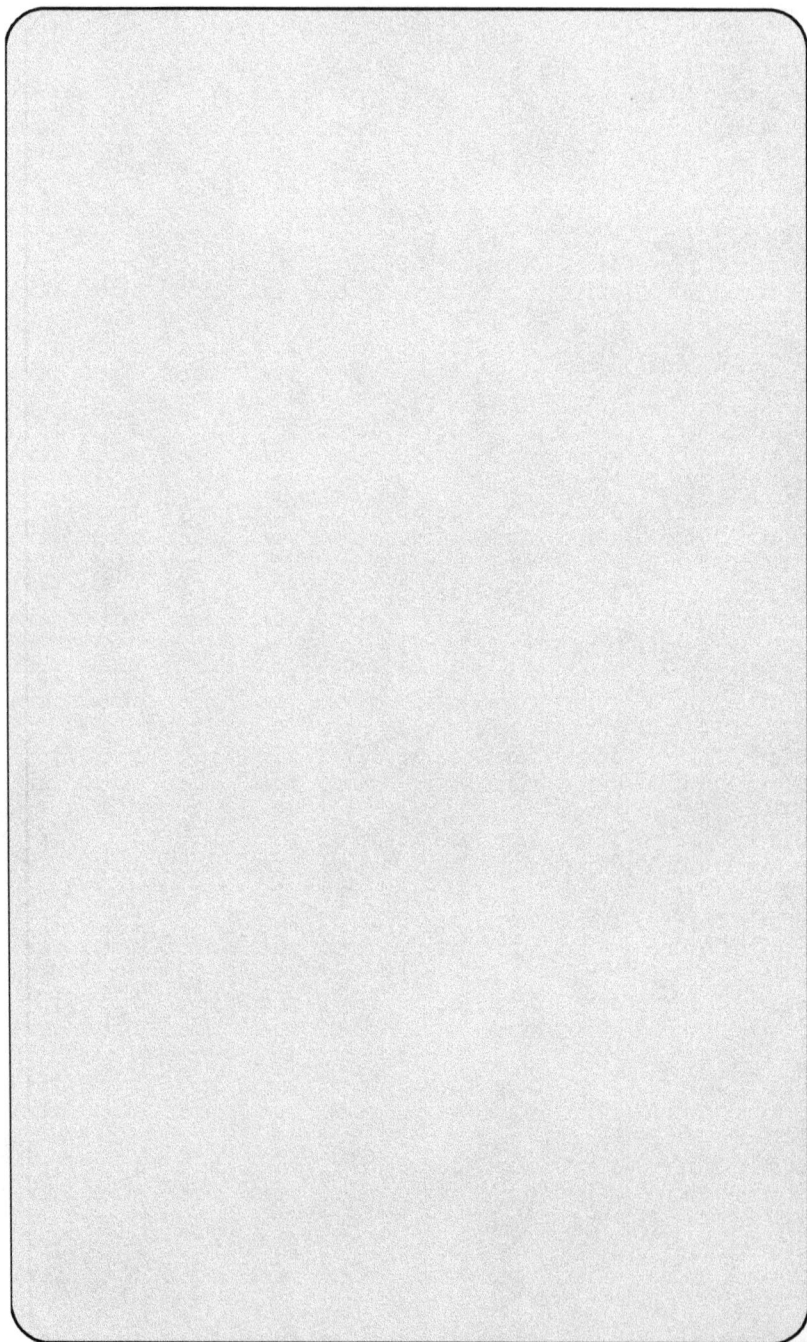

This is our ____ Anniversary, celebrated in ____

This is our ____ Anniversary, celebrated in ____

This is our ____ Anniversary, celebrated in ____

This is our ____ Anniversary, celebrated in ____

This is our ____ Anniversary, celebrated in ____

This is our ____ Anniversary, celebrated in ____

This is our ＿＿＿ Anniversary, celebrated in ＿＿＿

This is our ____ Anniversary, celebrated in ____

This is our ____ Anniversary, celebrated in ____

This is our ____ Anniversary, celebrated in ____

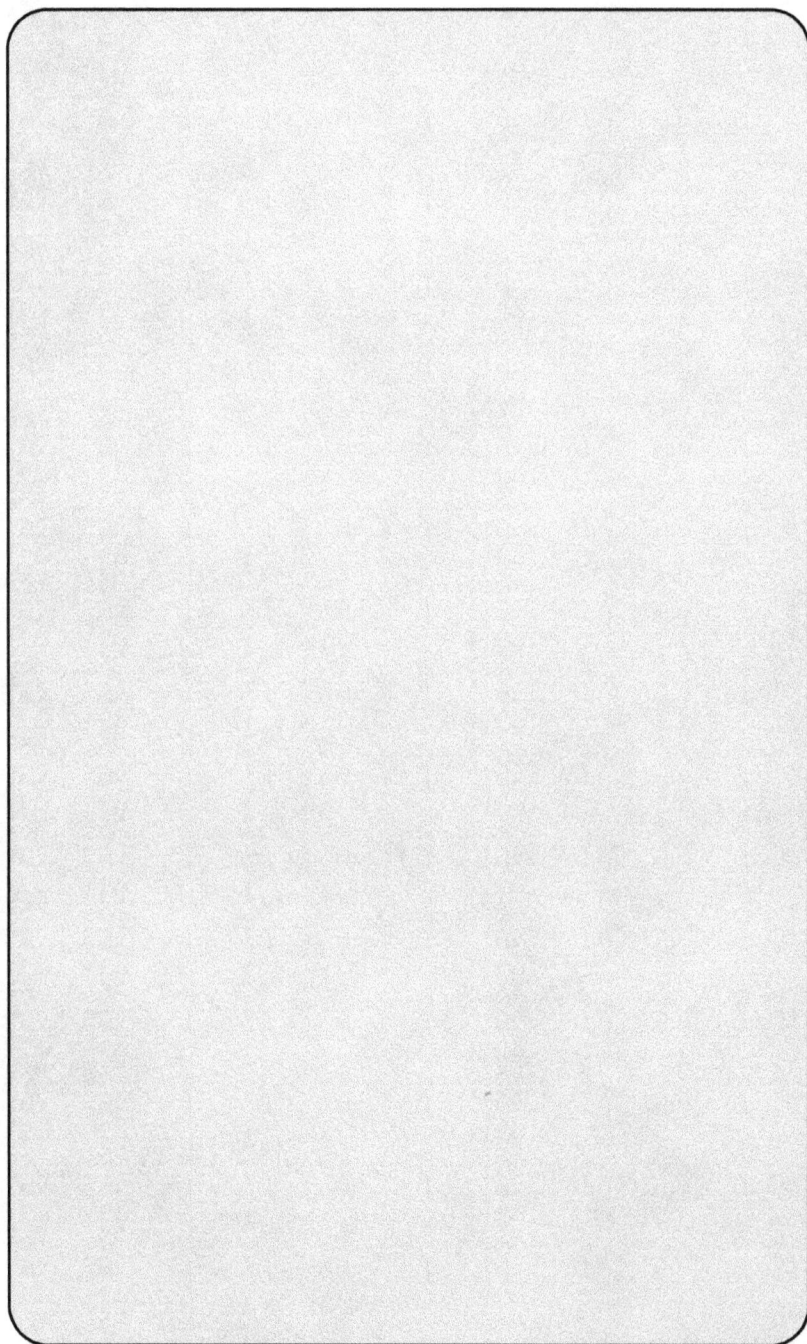

This is our ____ Anniversary, celebrated in ____

This is our ____ Anniversary, celebrated in ____

This is our ____ Anniversary, celebrated in ____

This is our ____ Anniversary, celebrated in ____

This is our ____ Anniversary, celebrated in ____

This is our ____ Anniversary, celebrated in ____

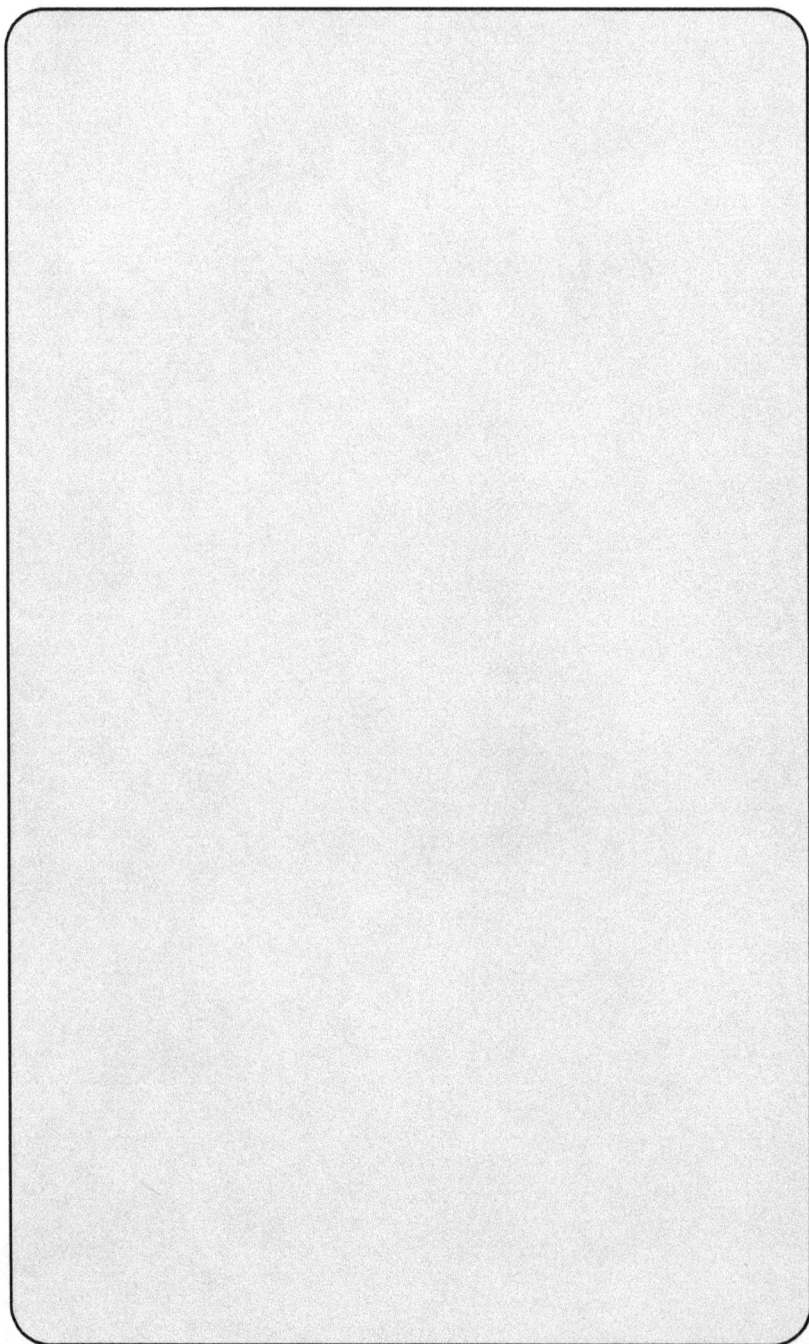

This is our ____ Anniversary, celebrated in ____

This is our ____ Anniversary, celebrated in ____

This is our ____ Anniversary, celebrated in ____

This is our ____ Anniversary, celebrated in ____

This is our ____ Anniversary, celebrated in ____

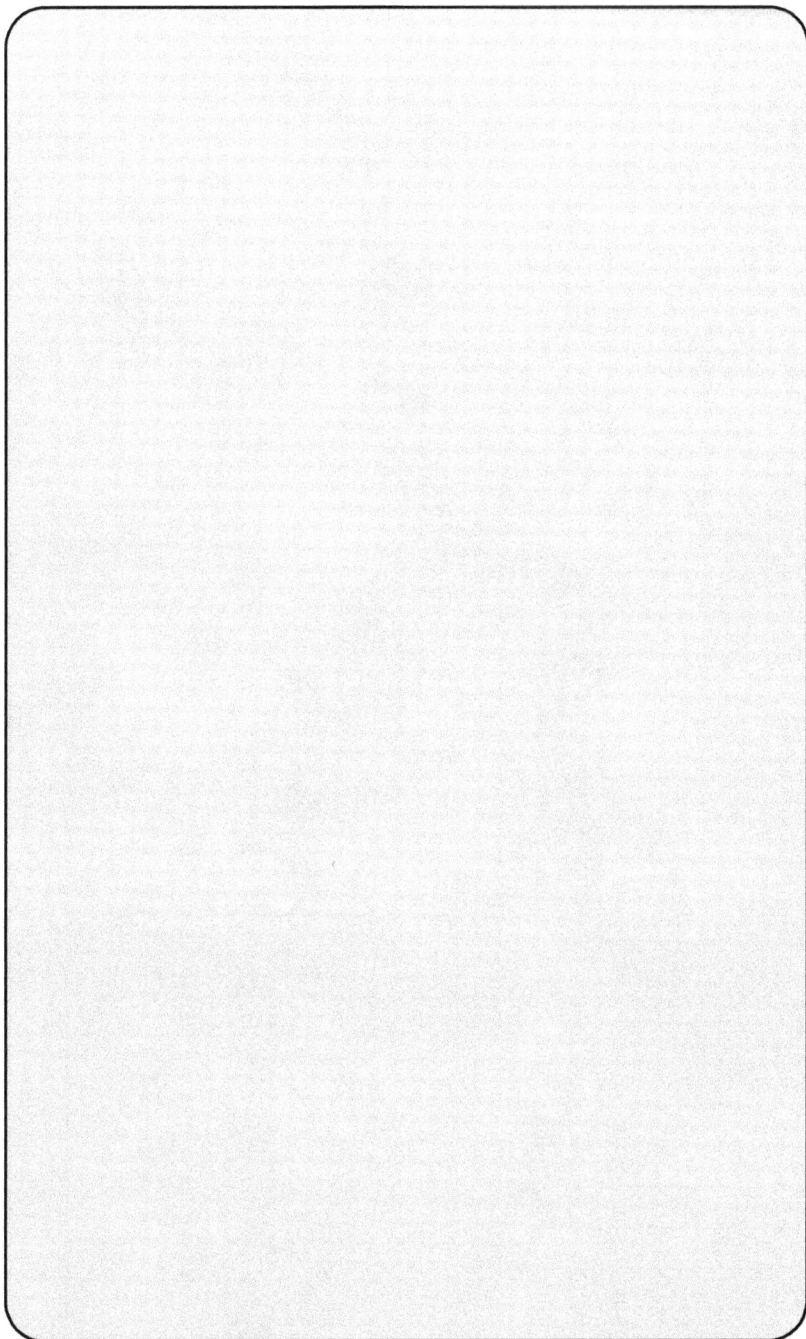

This is our ____ Anniversary, celebrated in ____

This is our ____ Anniversary, celebrated in ____

This is our ____ Anniversary, celebrated in ____

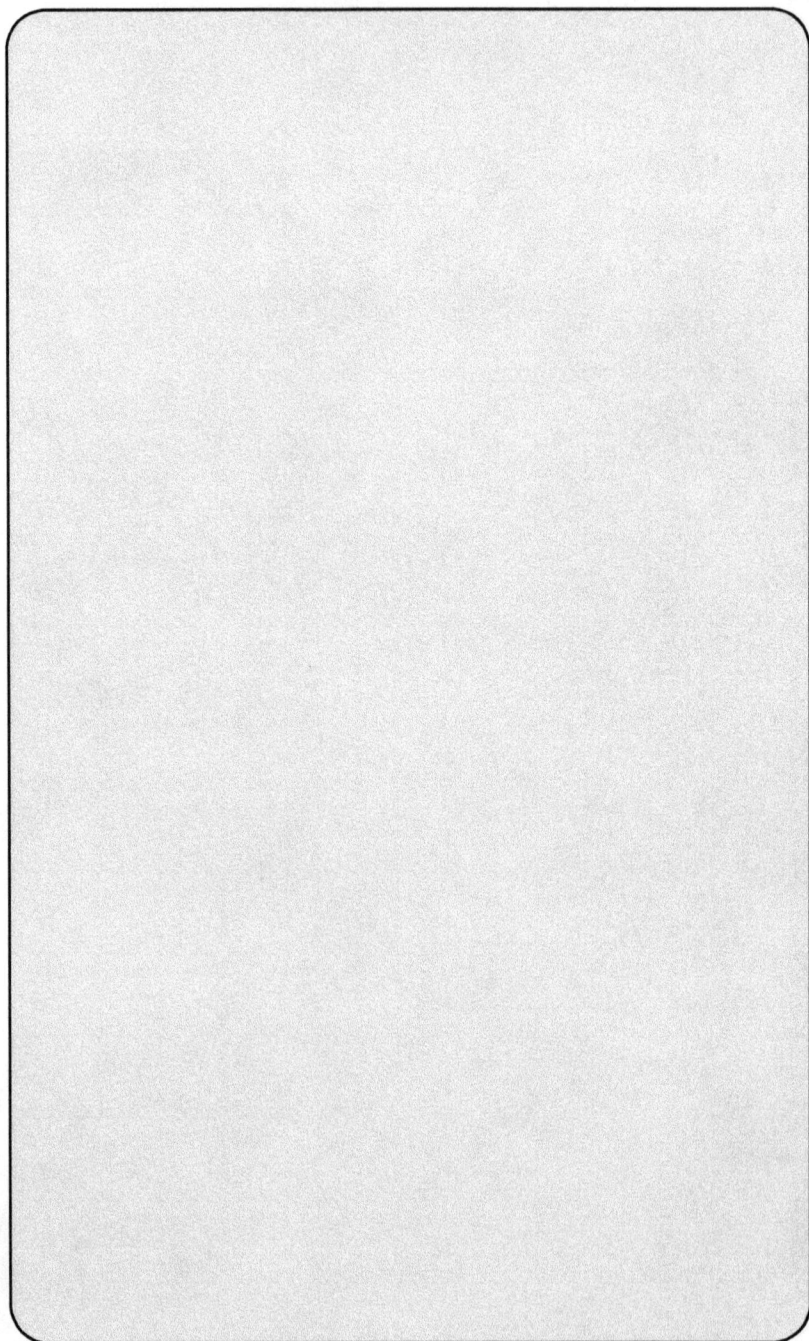

This is our ____ Anniversary, celebrated in ____

This is our ____ Anniversary, celebrated in ____

This is our ____ Anniversary, celebrated in ____

This is our ____ Anniversary, celebrated in ____

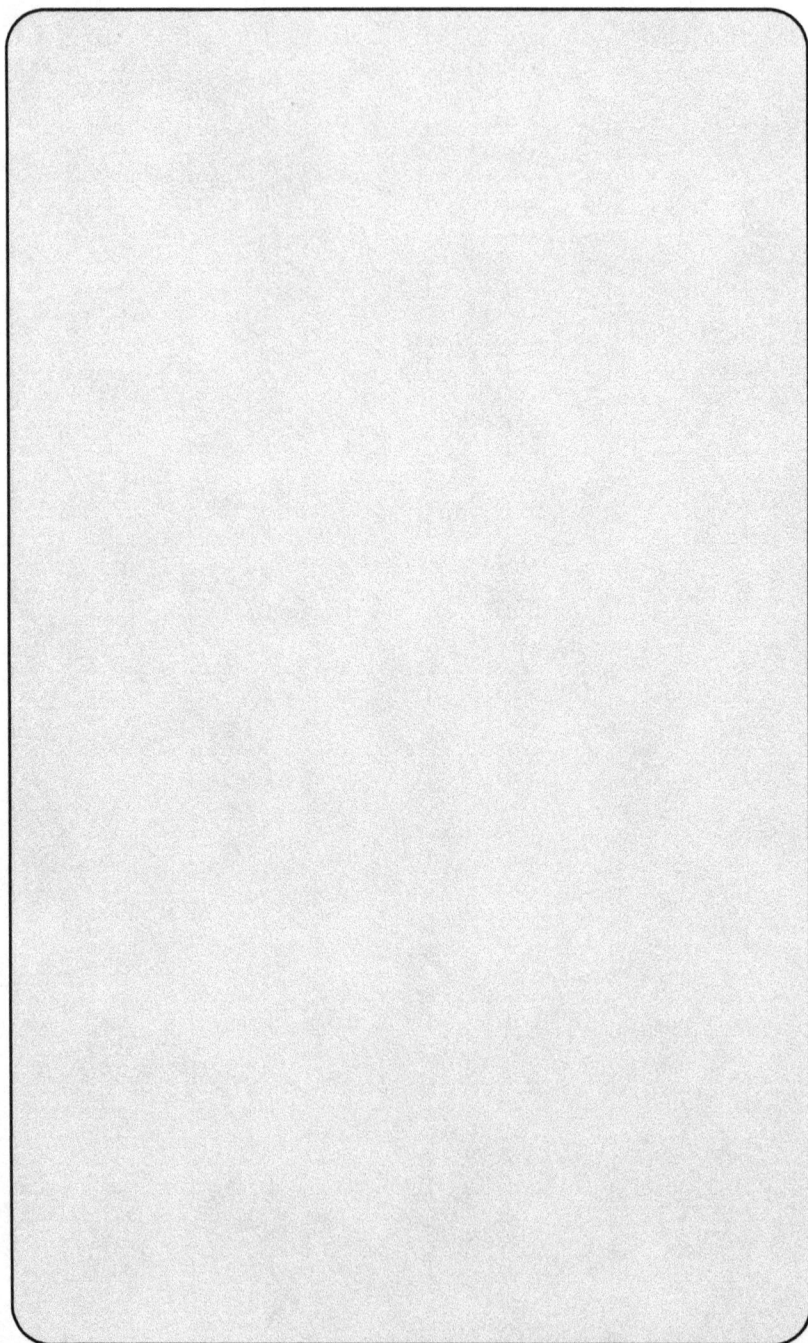

This is our ____ Anniversary, celebrated in ____

This is our ____ Anniversary, celebrated in ____

This is our ____ Anniversary, celebrated in ____

This is our ____ Anniversary, celebrated in ____

This is our ____ Anniversary, celebrated in ____

This is our ____ Anniversary, celebrated in ____

This is our ＿＿＿ Anniversary, celebrated in ＿＿＿

This is our ____ Anniversary, celebrated in ____

This is our ____ Anniversary, celebrated in ____

This is our ____ Anniversary, celebrated in ____

This is our ____ Anniversary, celebrated in ____

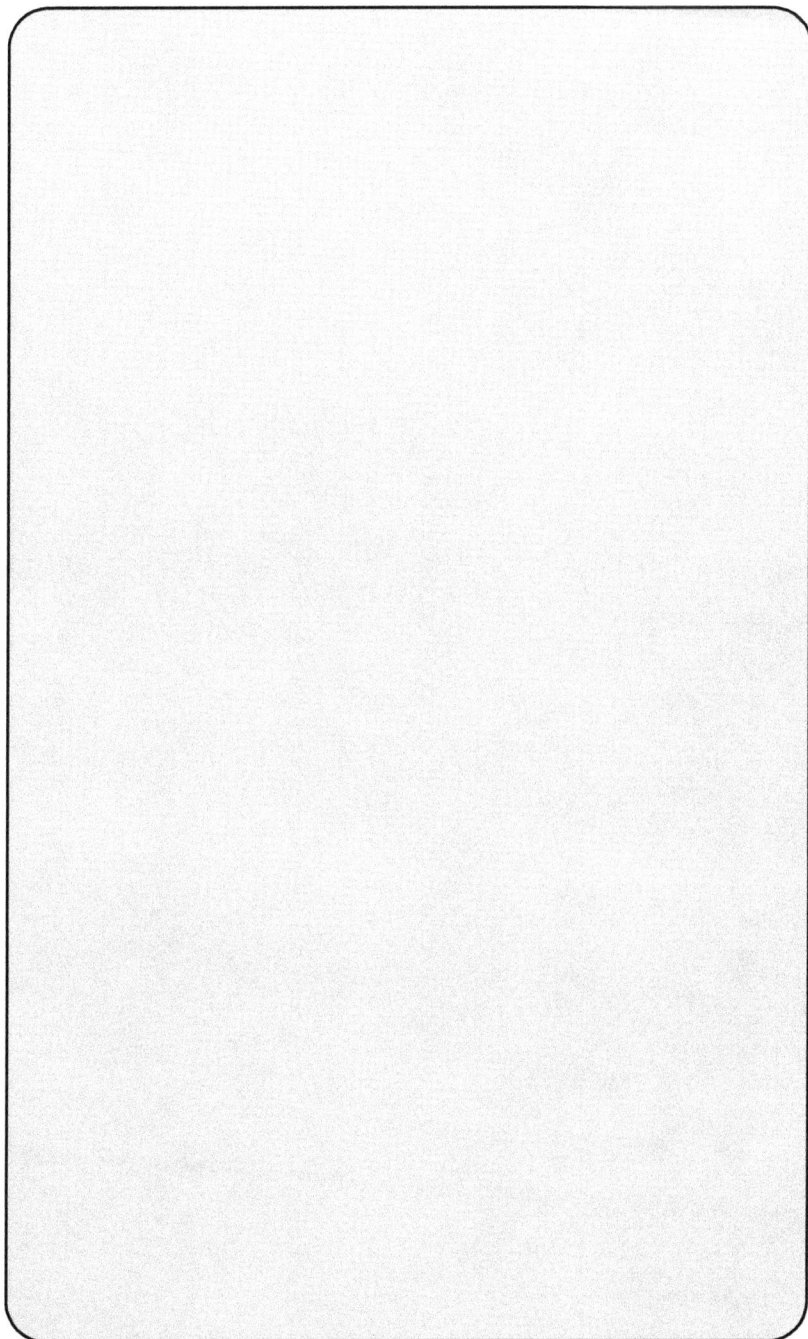

This is our ____ Anniversary, celebrated in ____

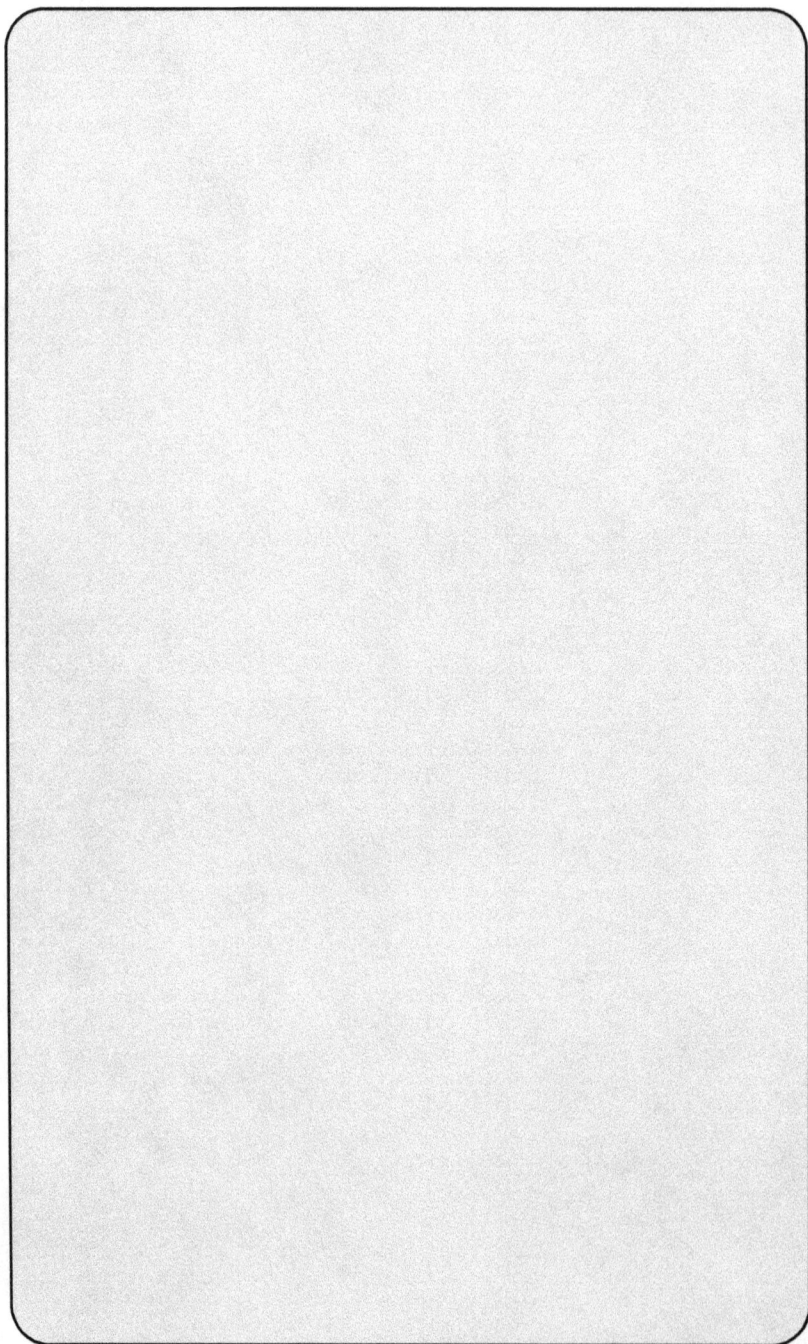

This is our ____ Anniversary, celebrated in ____

This is our ____ Anniversary, celebrated in ____

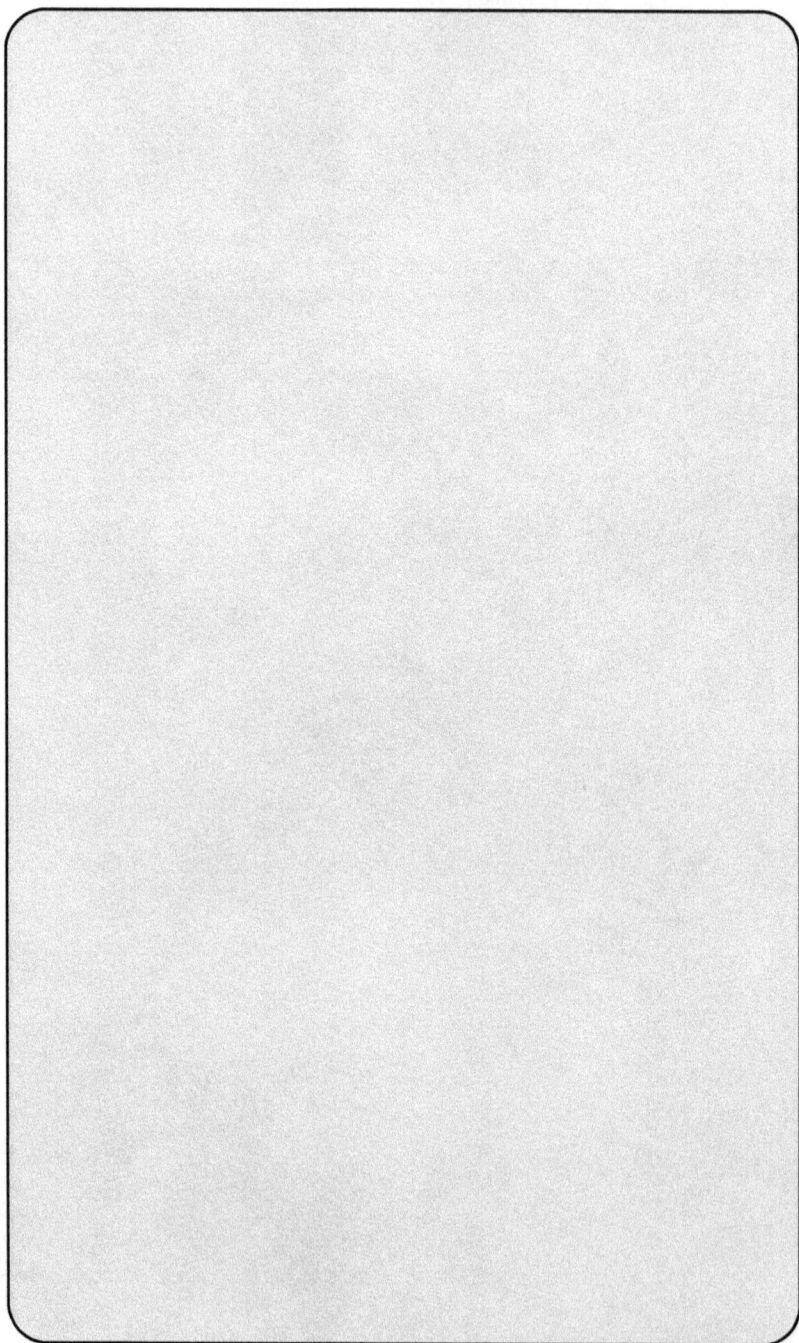

This is our ____ Anniversary, celebrated in ____

This is our ____ Anniversary, celebrated in ____

This is our ____ Anniversary, celebrated in ____

This is our ____ Anniversary, celebrated in ____

This is our ____ Anniversary, celebrated in ____

This is our ____ Anniversary, celebrated in ____

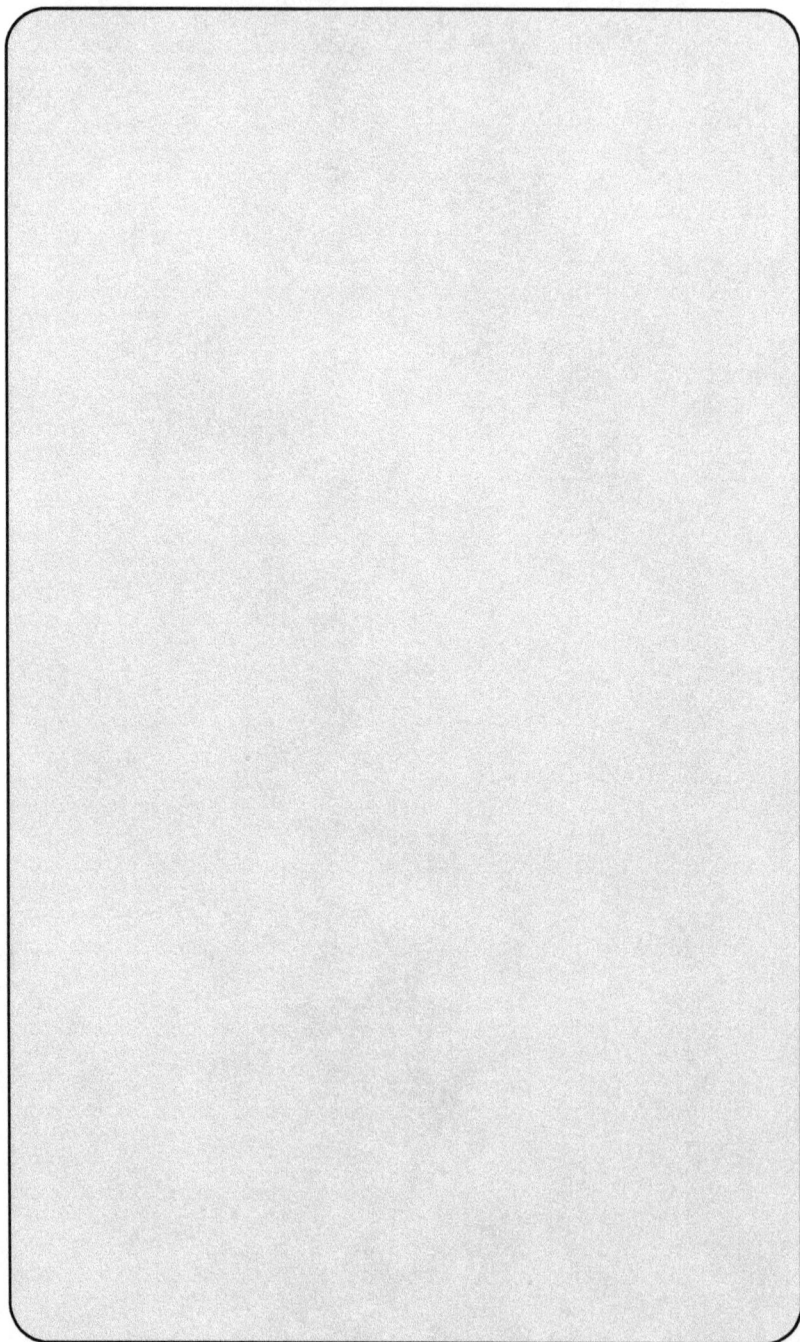

This is our ____ Anniversary, celebrated in ____

This is our ____ Anniversary, celebrated in ____

This is our ____ Anniversary, celebrated in ____

This is our ____ Anniversary, celebrated in ____

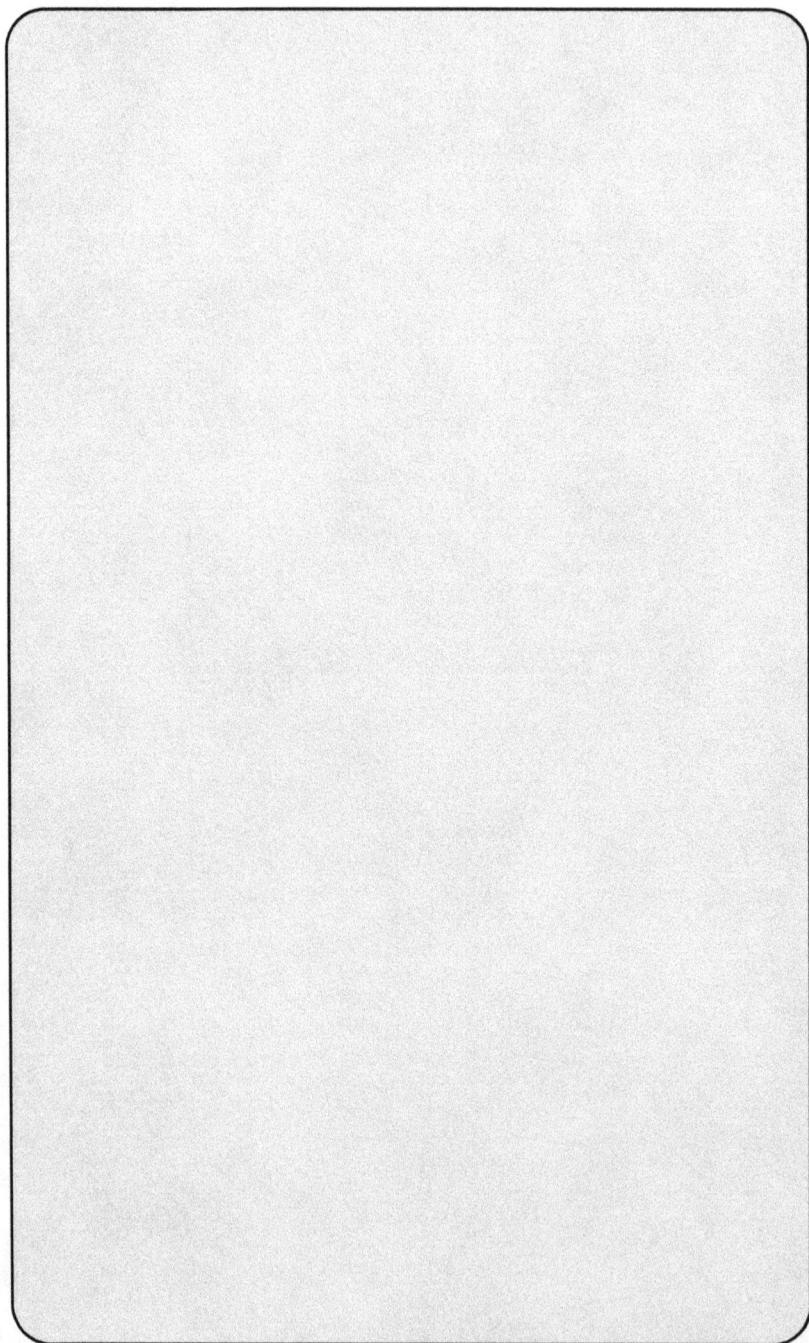

This is our ____ Anniversary, celebrated in ____

This is our ____ Anniversary, celebrated in ____

This is our ____ Anniversary, celebrated in ____

This is our _ _ _ _ Anniversary, celebrated in _ _ _ _

This is our ____ Anniversary, celebrated in ____

This is our ____ Anniversary, celebrated in ____

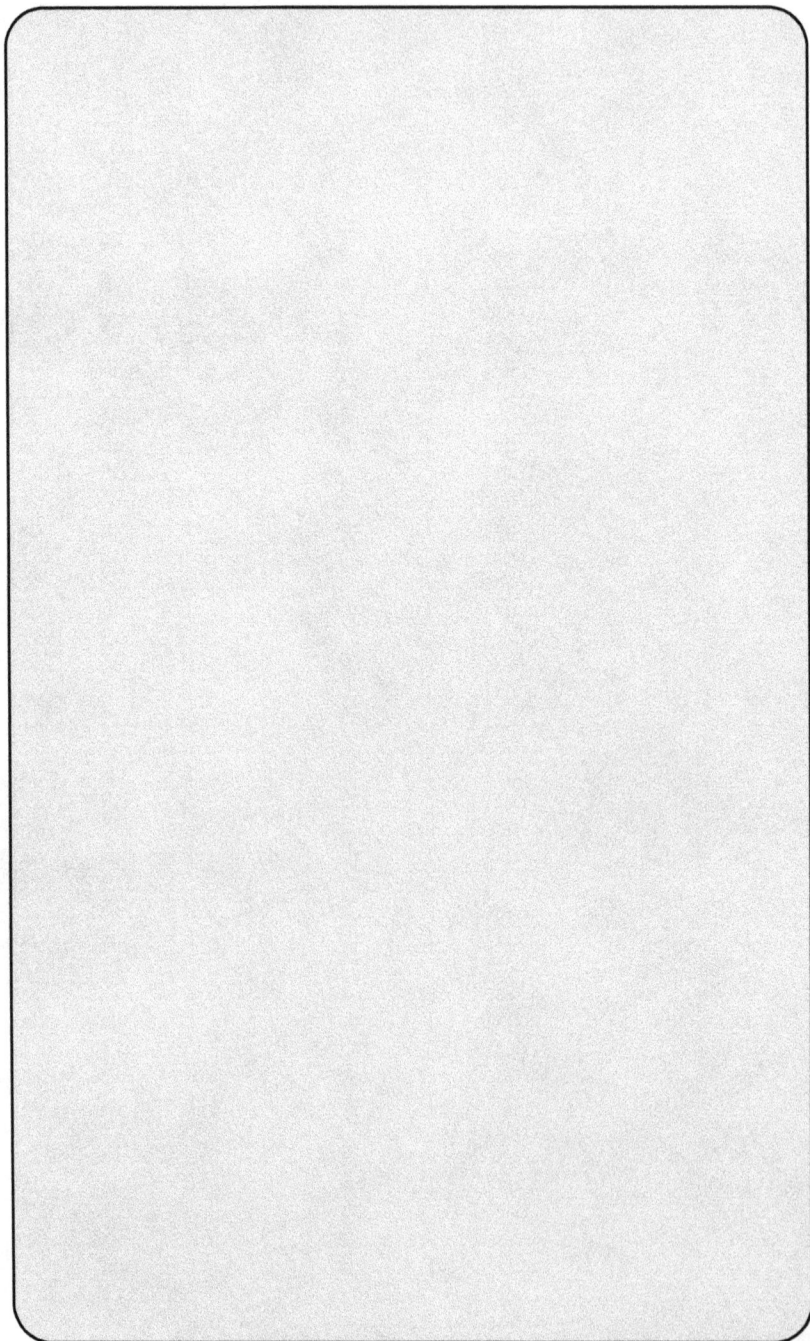

This is our ____ Anniversary, celebrated in ____

This is our ____ Anniversary, celebrated in ____

This is our ____ Anniversary, celebrated in ____

This is our ____ Anniversary, celebrated in ____

This is our ____ Anniversary, celebrated in ____

This is our ____ Anniversary, celebrated in ____

This is our ____ Anniversary, celebrated in ____

This is our ____ Anniversary, celebrated in ____

This is our ____ Anniversary, celebrated in ____

This is our ____ Anniversary, celebrated in ____

This is our ____ Anniversary, celebrated in ____

This is our ____ Anniversary, celebrated in ____

This is our ____ Anniversary, celebrated in ____

This is our ____ Anniversary, celebrated in ____

This is our ____ Anniversary, celebrated in ____

This is our ____ Anniversary, celebrated in ____

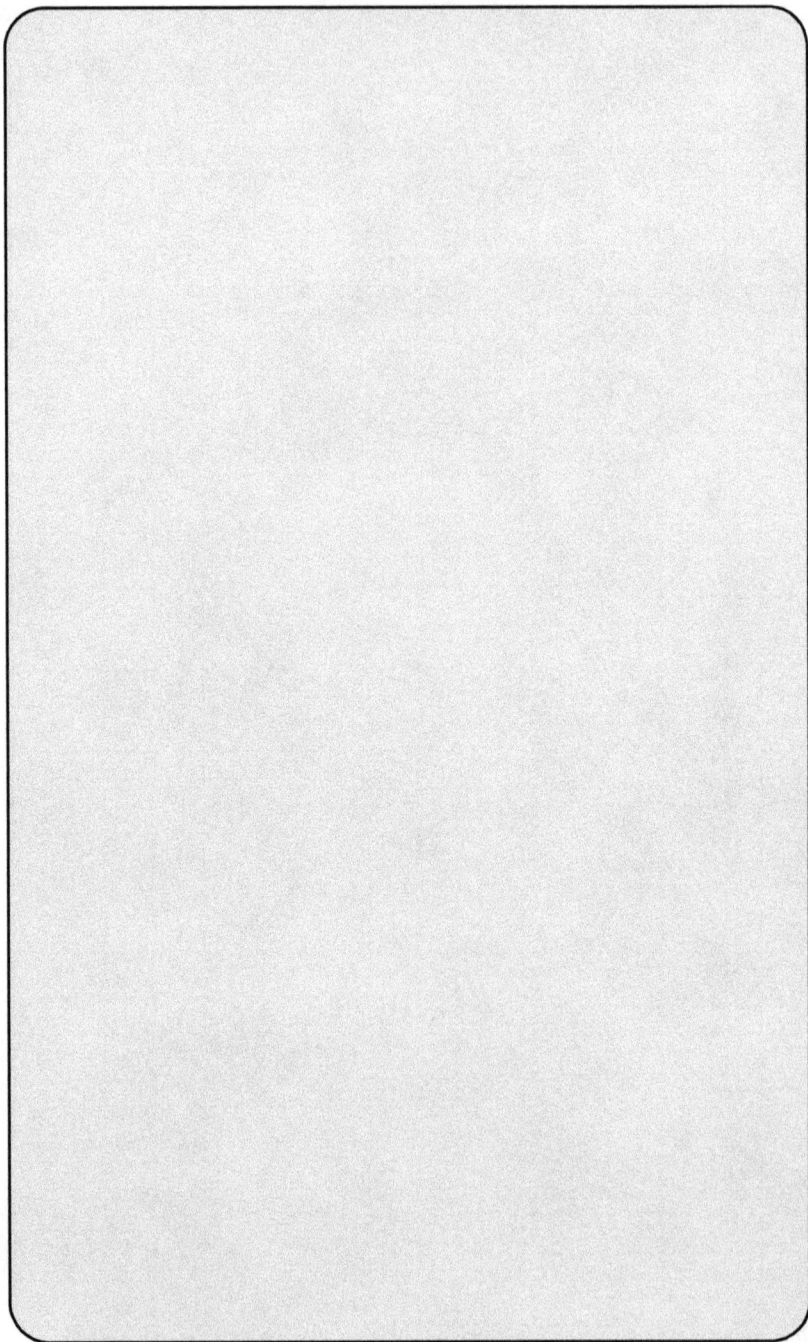

This is our ____ Anniversary, celebrated in ____

This is our ____ Anniversary, celebrated in ____

This is our ____ Anniversary, celebrated in ____

This is our ____ Anniversary, celebrated in ____

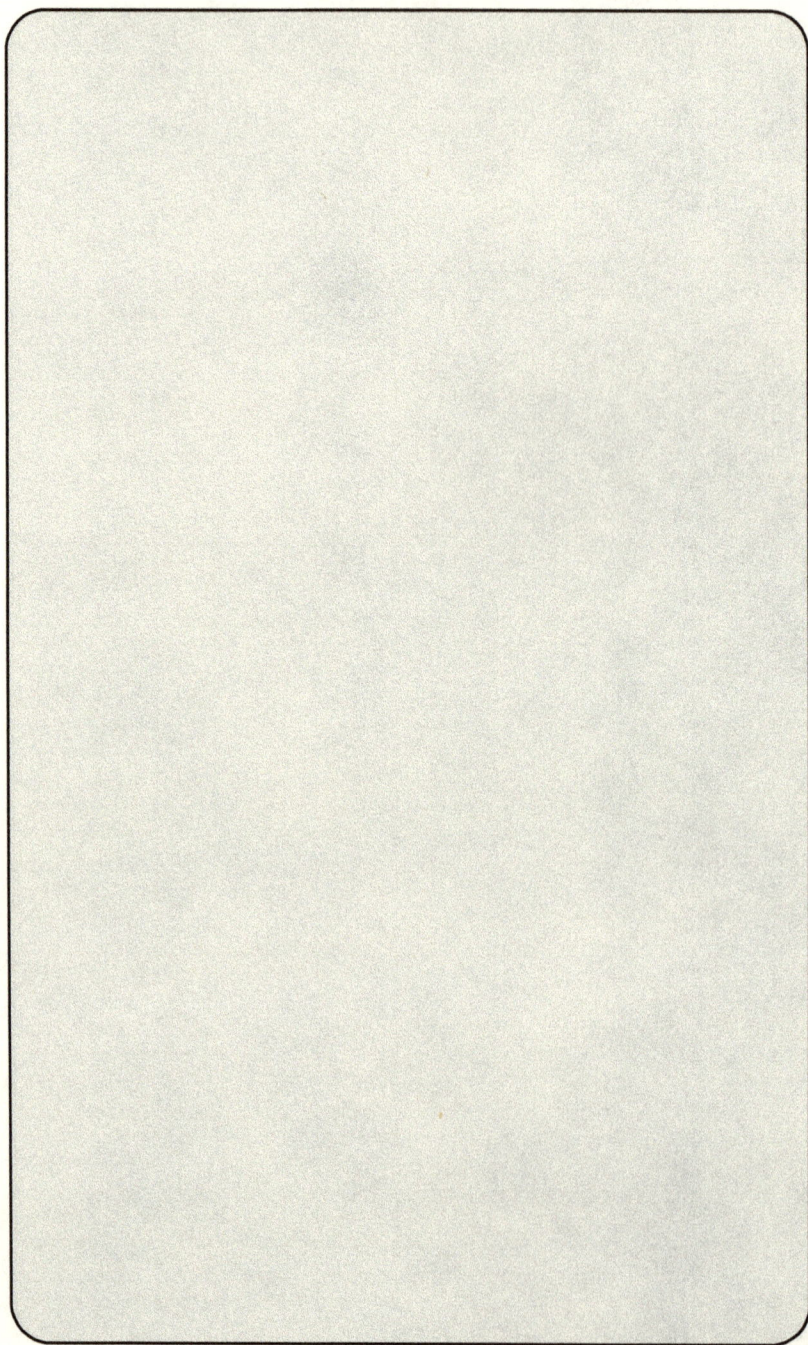

This is our ____ Anniversary, celebrated in ____

This is our ____ Anniversary, celebrated in ____

This is our ____ Anniversary, celebrated in ____

This is our ____ Anniversary, celebrated in ____

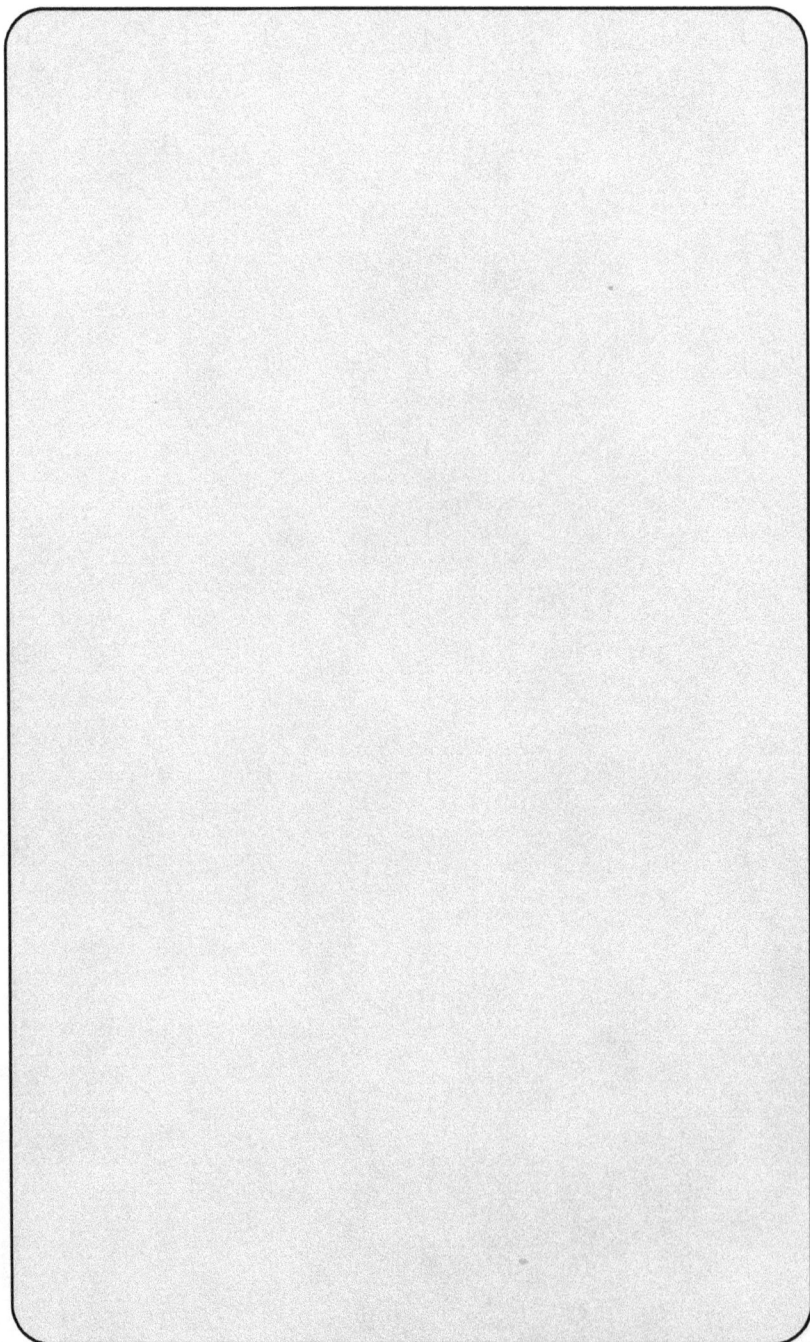

This is our ____ Anniversary, celebrated in ____

This is our ____ Anniversary, celebrated in ____

This is our ____ Anniversary, celebrated in ____

This is our ____ Anniversary, celebrated in ____

This is our ____ Anniversary, celebrated in ____

This is our ____ Anniversary, celebrated in ____

This is our ____ Anniversary, celebrated in ____

This is our ____ Anniversary, celebrated in ____

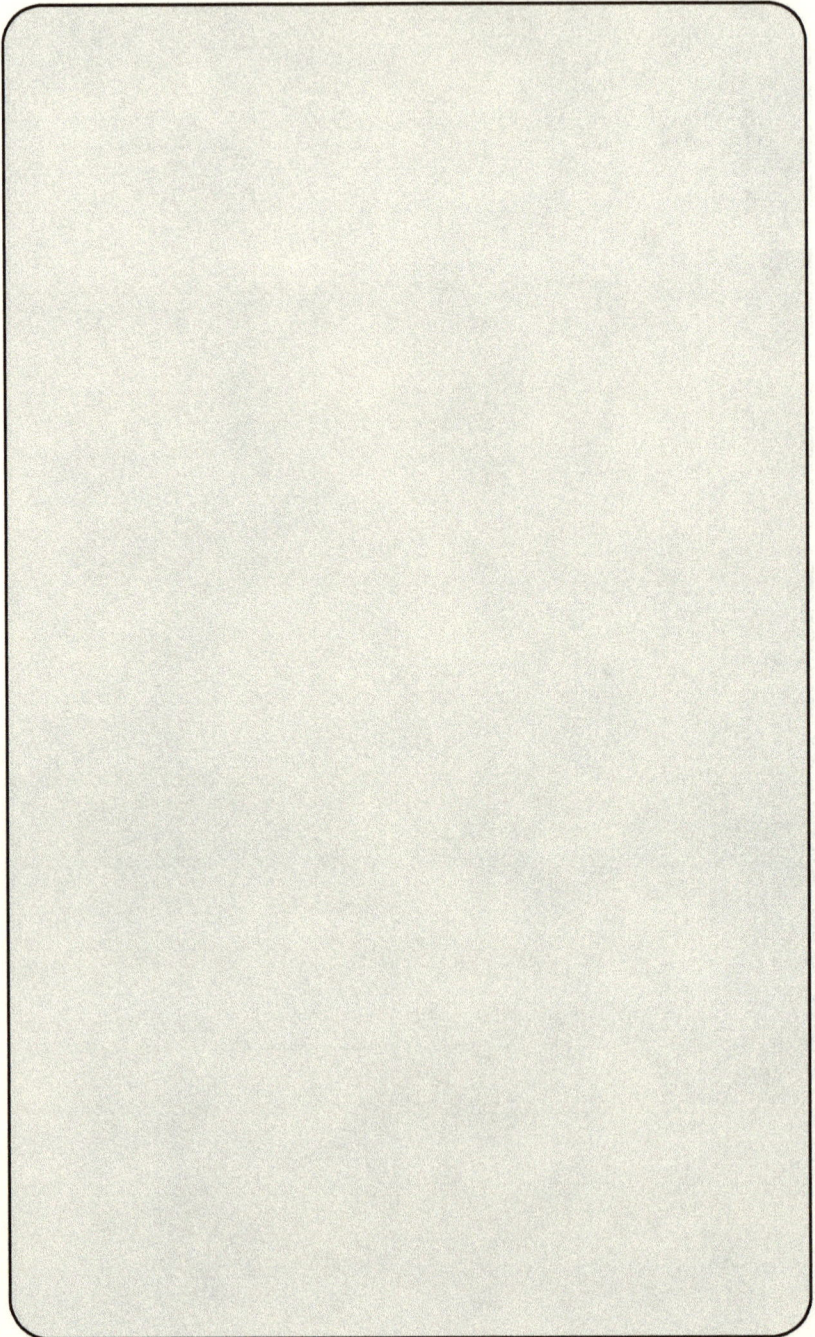

This is our ____ Anniversary, celebrated in ____

This is our ____ Anniversary, celebrated in ____

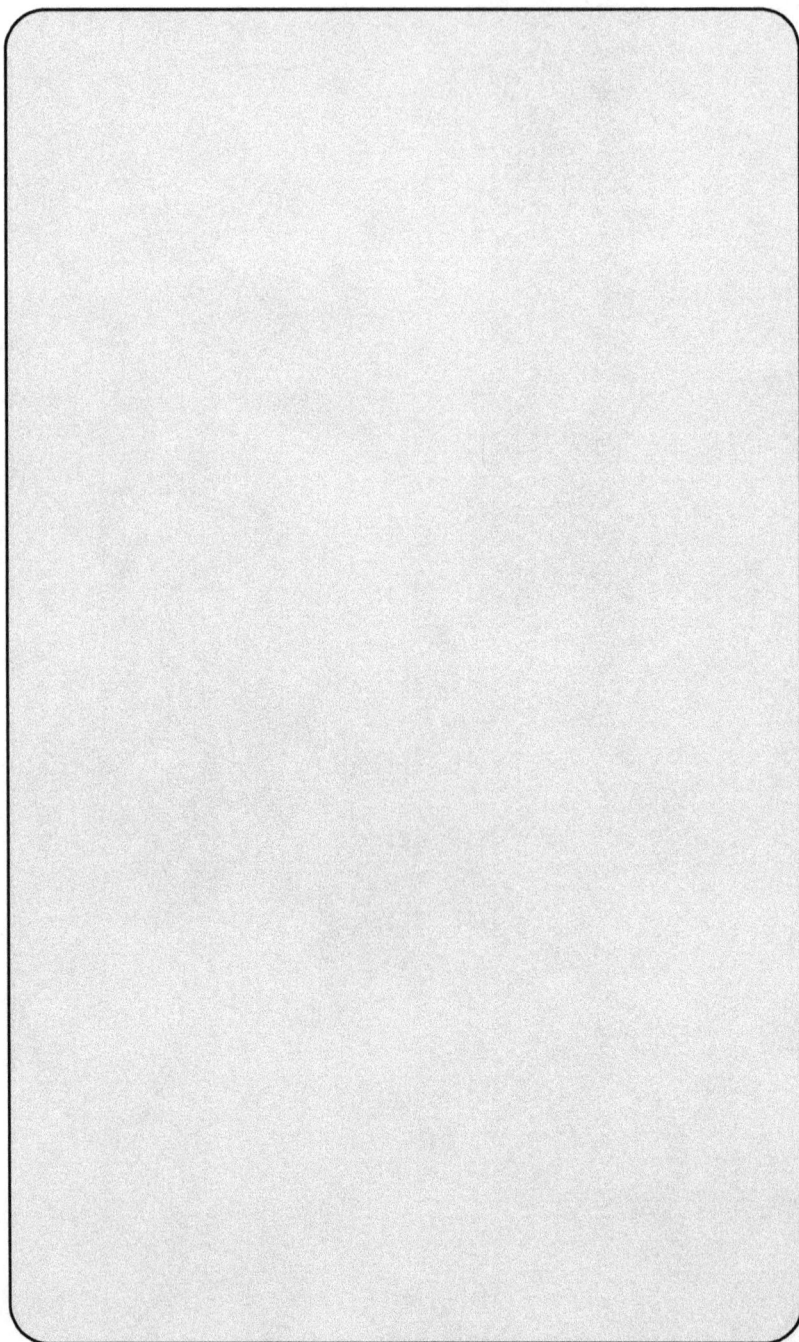

This is our ____ Anniversary, celebrated in ____

This is our ____ Anniversary, celebrated in ____

This is our ____ Anniversary, celebrated in ____

This is our ____ Anniversary, celebrated in ____

This is our ____ Anniversary, celebrated in ____

www.ingramcontent.com/pod-product-compliance
Lightning Source LLC
Chambersburg PA
CBHW031325040426
42443CB00005B/220